Top Secret

Sky Marshals

Mark Beyer

HIGH
interest
books

Children's Press®
A Division of Scholastic Inc.
New York / Toronto / London / Auckland / Sydney
Mexico City / New Delhi / Hong Kong
Danbury, Connecticut

Book Design: Erica Clendening and Michelle Innes
Contributing Editor: Jennifer Silate

Photo Credits: Cover, p. 22 © AFP/Corbis; p. 4 © SuperStock, Inc.; p. 7 © Jan Halaska/Index Stock Imagery, Inc.; p. 8 © Alan Schein Photography/Corbis; p. 13 © Wally McNamee/Corbis; pp. 15, 21, 24, 29 © Reuters NewMedia Inc./Corbis; pp. 16, 27, 30, 34, 37, 41 © AP/Wide World Photos; p. 19 © Bob Krist/Corbis

Library of Congress Cataloging-in-Publication Data

Beyer, Mark (Mark T.)
  Sky marshals / Mark Beyer.
  p. cm. — (Top secret)
  Includes bibliographical references and index.
  Contents: Introduction — Passenger protection — Sky marshal qualifications — Training — Guns in the air : benefit or added danger?
  ISBN 0-516-24314-4 (lib. bdg.) — ISBN 0-516-24377-2 (pbk.)
  1. Hijacking of aircraft—Prevention—Juvenile literature. 2. Sky marshals—United States—Juvenile literature. 3. Air travel—Safety measures—Juvenile literature. 4. Terrorism—Prevention—Juvenile literature. [1. Sky marshals. 2. Hijacking of aircraft—Prevention. 3. Air travel—Safety measures.]   I. Title. II. Series: Top secret (New York, N.Y.)

HE9803.Z7H525 2003
363.28'76—dc21

                                            2002009171

Contents

Introduction   5

1   Agents in the Air   9

2   Having What It Takes   17

3   The Making of a Sky Marshal   23

4   Safety in the Skies   35

New Words   42

For Further Reading   44

Resources   45

Index   47

About the Author   48

Introduction

Imagine sitting on an airplane during a cross-country flight. Maybe you're going on vacation with your family or to visit a friend. The plane is cruising at 35,000 feet (10,668 meters), and you have just opened up your favorite book. Suddenly, you see two men get out of their seats and walk toward the door of the cockpit. One man bangs on the door. The other turns around in the aisle, looks angrily at the passengers, and raises a gun in the air. He yells, "We're taking over this plane! Everyone keep quiet and no one will get hurt!" Then the cockpit door opens and the other man rushes in. You and your fellow passengers have just been hijacked.

As rare as this scenario is, hundreds of people around the world have experienced it. Everyone has ideas about what he or she would do in such

Sometimes, a ride through the friendly skies can be dangerous. Sky marshals are ready to act when danger strikes.

a situation: Should I rush the hijacker and try to take away his or her weapon? Should I sit silently and let the hijackers take the airplane where they want?

You may be asking yourself another question: Can anyone stop a hijacking? The answer is "yes." On planes around the world, sky marshals are calming passengers' fears by working to make airplane travel safe.

Sky marshals have been at work in the United States since the 1960s. They are highly trained agents who are prepared to defend a plane against hijackers. Sky marshals work undercover. None of the other passengers on a plane know who the sky marshals are. When a threat is made to the safety of the plane and its passengers, sky marshals swiftly spring into action. Let's take a look at the sky marshals of the United States.

Is there a sky marshal on this plane?
An undercover sky marshal is hard to
pick out of a crowd.

Chapter One

Agents in the Air

The first time an airplane hijacking occurred was in 1931 in Peru. By the 1960s, hijackings started to happen more often. Because of very few security precautions, taking control of an airplane was fairly easy. There were no metal detectors used at check-in gates to find guns, knives, or bombs on people or in baggage. If someone was determined to hijack an airplane, that person could easily sneak a gun or other weapon onto the plane.

In the 1960s, most hijacked planes were going to, and coming from, places such as Europe, Mexico, the Caribbean, South America, and the Middle East. Hijackings were often committed by people who wanted to protest against war or express their political opinions. These hijackers got world-wide attention for themselves and their causes.

As airline security gets tighter, the lines that passengers must wait in before boarding their plane get longer.

Such crimes were extremely dangerous to the innocent passengers on board because the hijackers did not fear losing their own lives.

CLASSIFIED INFORMATION

The first hijacking in the United States occurred on May 1, 1961. The plane was hijacked in Florida and flown to Cuba. That year, there were four hijackings to Cuba.

Sky Marshals

Airline safety is important. Passengers expect to be flown safely from one city to another. In 1968, the U.S. government decided to create the Sky Marshal program after several airplanes were hijacked from the United States to Cuba in previous years. The role of the sky marshal was to ride on planes to stop hijackings to and from Cuba. They traveled in secret and carried guns. However, not every plane carried a sky marshal. Hijackers could not know which planes would have a sky marshal and which wouldn't. The U.S. government hoped that the possibility that a plane might have a sky marshal on it would stop hijackers. Over time, fewer and fewer hijackings were attempted.

As the number of hijackings decreased, so did the number of sky marshals patrolling the skies. In 1971, President Richard Nixon cut the Sky Marshal program by 66 percent. The government started using other ways to try to stop hijackings and make airplane travel safer. By 1973, all airports used metal detectors to check passengers and their bags before letting them on an airplane.

A Rise in Hijackings

In 1985, Islamic terrorists hijacked TWA flight 847 out of Athens, Greece. They held the plane on the ground for fifteen days. The terrorists killed one passenger, U.S. Navy scuba diver Robert Stethem.

THE LEGEND OF DAN COOPER

Many of the hijackings in the 1960s and 1970s were political protests. There was at least one hijacker, however, who hijacked a plane simply for the money. A man who called himself Dan Cooper hijacked a plane leaving Portland, Oregon, bound for the Seattle-Tacoma International Airport (Sea-Tac). Cooper claimed to be carrying a bomb. When he opened his suitcase to get something out, a flight attendant saw some red cylinders and wires inside. Cooper demanded a ransom of $200,000. When the plane landed at Sea-Tac, he was given the money. Then he demanded that the plane be flown to Mexico. The authorities gave in to his demands. Everyone was let off of the plane except the flight crew and a flight attendant. During the flight to Mexico, however, he put on a parachute and jumped from the plane's rear stairway 10,000 feet above the ground. At the time, the plane was flying over the deep pine forests of eastern Washington State, in the middle of a snowstorm! The Federal Bureau of Investigation (FBI) searched the area where they believed he would have landed. No evidence of any kind was found to prove if Cooper had landed safely and gotten away, or died during his dramatic escape. Cooper's hijacking led to a change in the way planes are designed. The back stairway door can no longer be opened during a flight. The device that keeps the door closed is called a Cooper Vane.

Ronald Reagan's Federal
Air Marshal program
really took off.

After this incident, President Ronald Reagan helped create the Federal Air Marshal (FAM) program. The program was created to put sky marshals on more flights. Instead of just stopping hijackings to only Cuba, the new sky marshals would ride international flights to areas that were considered high risks for hijackings.

September 11, 2001

The morning of September 11, 2001, changed everyone's view of hijackings. Four airplanes from Boston, Massachusetts, and Newark, New Jersey, were hijacked. Of course, none of the passengers boarding those flights that morning knew the planes were going to be used as bombs to target buildings in New York City and Washington, D.C.—none except the hijackers. Everyone on both planes died, and so did about 3,000 people in the buildings and on the ground. The twin towers of the World Trade Center in New York City were totally demolished. The Pentagon in Washington, D.C., was badly damaged. It was the worst hijacking disaster in history.

On September 11, only thirty-two sky marshals were at work. All of them were on international flights, traveling to foreign cities. Unfortunately, the four planes that were hijacked on September 11 were all flying to cities in the United States. After the destruction of the World Trade Center towers and the Pentagon, the government rapidly began to develop new ideas for airline safety.

People's fears soared after September 11, 2001. Flight safety became a huge concern.

Chapter Two

Having What It Takes

On September 20, 2001, President George W. Bush announced that he would expand the FAM program. He hopes the program will stop future hijackings. Just as they were used after the 1985 hijacking of flight 847, sky marshals were once again relied on to make plane travel safer.

Help Wanted

The Transportation Security Administration (TSA) was formed months after the tragic events of September 11. The TSA hired twenty-eight thousand passenger and baggage screeners in an effort to keep bombs and hijackers off of planes. The TSA also works with the Federal Aviation Authority (FAA) on the Federal Air Marshal program. The TSA hires the sky marshals, and the FAA schedules the marshals on

After the attacks on the Pentagon (shown left) and the World Trade Center, the U.S. government turned to sky marshals to make air travel safe again.

flights. About 150,000 people applied to be sky marshals after September 11. The number of sky marshals that will be hired is being kept a secret.

Sky marshal training and flight assignments are very secretive operations. Federal officials don't want potential terrorists and hijackers to find out details of their operations. What isn't a secret is that the new sky marshals will be some of the most highly trained airline security that the United States has ever had.

Sky Marshal Requirements

There are many requirements a candidate must meet to become a sky marshal. A sky marshal must be a U.S. citizen, under forty years old, and able to get top-secret security clearance. Top-secret clearance is given only to those people who have not been arrested for serious crimes. Those applying for a job as a sky marshal must pass a complete background check. Using drugs, associating with criminals, or having bad credit will prevent an applicant from becoming a sky marshal.

Other requirements for becoming a sky marshal include three years' experience in a similar job, such as police officer, federal agent, or member of the U.S. military. Sky marshals must also submit to

Many sky marshal recruits have already gone through boot camp or other military training.

random drug and alcohol tests. Finally, every sky marshal must be an expert shooter with a pistol.

CLASSIFIED INFORMATION

A beginner sky marshal is paid at least $35,100 a year. More experienced sky marshals can make as much as $80,800.

The New Sky Marshals

The TSA is on the hunt for new sky marshals. Whom will they choose? As women are being given a more active role in federal, state, and local law enforcement groups, they will also be welcomed in the new FAM program. Experts have guessed that both men and women will be used as sky marshals. The FAM looks for people who can blend in with a crowd. They want people who look, and can act, like an average airline passenger. A hijacker looking out for big, strong men will be easily subdued if a small, but well-trained man or woman who looks like the other passengers suddenly surprises him or her!

After September 11, 2001, security tightened in airports around the world. In addition to undercover sky marshals, uniformed agents were hired to keep airline passengers safe.

Chapter Three — The Making of a Sky Marshal

Well-trained sky marshals are an important part of a successful airline security program. FAM training headquarters are in New Jersey. Recruits must complete a fourteen-week course. Sky marshal trainees must learn many things before they are ready to protect a plane full of passengers.

Sky marshals must be able to think and react quickly. This does not simply mean how fast they can pull out a gun and shoot a hijacker. Trainees spend time in a classroom learning basic law enforcement skills. These skills include criminal investigation, observation, suspect detection, and negotiation. Sky marshals must know what to expect during a hijacking—and be able to deal with any situation.

During the intense training, a sky marshal learns to act swiftly and safely when faced with danger.

Sharpshooters

A sky marshal must try to negotiate with a hijacker before using force. When force is needed, however, a

Sky marshals are responsible for the safety of the passengers on their flight. Every shot they take must hit its target.

sky marshal must be ready to act quickly. Sky marshal trainees learn how and when to fire their weapons. They learn these skills at shooting ranges.

One type of range is called a shoot-house. To simulate a real-life hijacking, the shoot-house is made to look like the inside of an airplane. Computer-controlled targets move up and down on all sides of a trainee as he or she walks through the range. A bulletproof observation tower lets trainers study and judge how well trainees perform. Trainees must learn to fire their weapon three times in 6 seconds. They must be able to shoot, reload, and shoot another three bullets in a total of 15 seconds. Sky marshals shoot three bullets at a time to make sure that they hit the hijacker. Sky marshals must learn how to shoot accurately while sitting and standing. They must also master spin moves to quickly hit someone coming from behind them. Sky marshals practice shooting for about 3 hours every week. They are some of the best shooters in U.S. law enforcement.

It is extremely important that marshals are expert shooters. If they miss their target, they could kill an innocent passenger or damage the plane, and cause the pilot to lose control of it.

An airplane flies at 35,000 feet (10,668 m). At that height, the air is very thin. There isn't enough oxygen in the air for people to breathe. Shooting a hole in an airplane could cause breathable air inside to escape, leaving only the thin air to breathe. To avoid damaging an airplane, sky marshals use hollow-point bullets. However, in some tests hollow-point bullets have gone through windows similar to those used on planes. Someday, sky marshals may use special bullets that turn into dust after hitting a solid surface. These bullets will still stop a hijacker and are less likely to damage a plane.

Too Close for Comfort

A 727 jet has a passenger cabin that is only 7 feet (2.1 m) tall and 10 feet (3 m) wide. The aisle is only

Testing is being done on special bullets that will take down a hijacker, but not the plane.

about 2 feet (0.6 m) wide. Trainees must know and be able to use self-defense and offensive hand-to-hand combat skills in this small space.

Trainees learn how to move quickly, react safely, and counter any move a hijacker could make inside a small airplane cabin. Trainees learn grabs, knee kicks, elbow punches, and other fighting techniques that will quickly stop a hijacker.

SKY | SKILLS

Sky marshal trainees learn how to use the radios and other controls in the plane's cockpit, in case something happens to the flight crew. Sky marshals must know how to find a bomb in a passenger's carry-on bag. They must also know where on the plane to put the bomb so that it will do the least amount of damage if it explodes.

Simulation Training

The skills trainees learn in the classroom and on the ranges are put to the test during simulation training. Simulation training takes place in an environment that is supposed to look and feel like reality. Trainees learn how to move, react, fire a weapon, and restrain a hijacker in an environment similar to the one they

In training, sky marshals learn to handle life-or-death situations in a cramped airplane cabin.

will face on the job. To simulate onboard events, the New Jersey FAM training facilities use an old B-727 narrow-body aircraft and an L-1011 wide-body aircraft. The facilities also have a five-story air traffic control tower where sky marshals train for ground-based missions.

Some airplanes carry hundreds of passengers. A sky marshal cannot know for sure where a hijacker will be seated or begin the hijacking. Trainees prepare for hijackings that start in any part of the plane.

Paintball guns add some color to sky marshal training.

In the Paint

Sometimes, sky marshals train with paintball guns. By firing paintball guns, the trainees learn how to react without risking anyone's life. A trainer posing as a hijacker sits among other trainers acting as passengers. In one scenario, the hijacker might spring up from a seat with a knife and grab a passenger. In another setting, the hijacker might pull a gun and rush toward the cockpit. Sometimes, several trainers act as hijackers.

Each of these scenarios presents different problems for sky marshal trainees. The trainees run through different scenarios over and over. At first, trainees may make mistakes. For example, they may shoot and hit passengers. They may also put the passengers in danger by hitting the plane. As the training progresses, these mistakes are eliminated.

Training with Computers

Computer simulations are also used to train sky marshals. These simulations use video scenarios of a mock hijacking. Scenes are projected onto huge screens in front of and behind a trainee as he or she sits in a mock airplane cabin. The scene changes, depending on the reaction of the trainee.

For example, the front screen may show a hijacker getting up from his seat. The hijacker grabs a female passenger and threatens to kill her with a knife. The trainee must spring into action. However, something is also going on in the rear of the plane. The trainee turns and sees two men with guns drawn coming down the aisle on the rear screen. The trainee fires at the men. One shot hits an attacker's shoulder. This is not a deadly shot, so the attacker keeps coming down the aisle. The trainee shoots several more shots. Finally both attackers fall. But wait! What about that hijacker with the knife? The trainee wheels around and finds the first attacker is right in front of him, holding the knife, making stabbing motions on-screen. The screen fades to black. The trainee has been killed.

CLASSIFIED INFORMATION

Some training simulators fire hard nylon balls at trainees to let them know when they have been shot. This helps to give the simulation a realistic feel—especially since the balls are fired forcefully and can even be painful!

Sky marshal training is intense. It has to be. If a sky marshal makes a mistake on a plane filled with passengers, hundreds of lives could be lost.

Chapter Four

Safety in the Skies

The U.S. government is spending billions of dollars to make flying safer. The TSA will add more security at airports by providing personnel and better screening equipment. They are turning to the latest technology to make flying as safe as possible. The TSA is testing X-ray scanners in airports around the country. These scanners can detect hidden objects beneath a person's clothes. They will allow airport security personnel to see if a person is carrying explosives or dangerous weapons. In the future, machines may be used that can scan a person's face or hand and match that scan to those of known terrorists. The TSA hopes that this technology will stop a hijacker from ever getting on a plane.

Airport authorities hope that tighter security and better technology will ground hijackers.

CLASSIFIED INFORMATION

There are more than 30,000 U.S. flights each day. It would take about 120,000 sky marshals to cover every flight. This would cost the government about $10 billion.

Patrolling the Skies

At least two sky marshals are assigned to a plane. One sky marshal must sit in first class so that he or she is between the passengers and the cockpit. Another marshal is most likely in the rear of the plane to watch over the passengers.

Most of the time, life as a sky marshal is routine. Marshals fly from place to place, eating airline food and waiting for something to happen. Some people argue that the government's money would be better

A sky marshal's job is made easier when knives, scissors, and other potentially dangerous objects are taken from passengers before they get on a plane.

used to improve technology for ground security rather than on training and hiring more sky marshals. They also worry that the gun a sky marshal carries could be used by a hijacker to take control of the airplane or to threaten the lives of passengers.

However, people in favor of having sky marshals on planes think that it is worth the risk if the marshal is well trained and an expert shooter. They also believe that even the threat of undercover, armed sky marshals on a plane is enough to stop a hijacker from attacking.

Armed...and Dangerous?

Many pilots want to be allowed to carry guns on the planes they fly. They hope to be able to protect themselves and their plane if there is no sky marshal on board. In May 2002, the TSA said that pilots could not carry guns. The TSA wanted the pilots to focus on flying the plane—not to be responsible for defending it against hijackers. The TSA was concerned that a gun in the cockpit could be taken and used by the hijacker. The TSA felt that stronger doors on the cockpit will protect the pilots and keep hijackers from the plane's controls so that guns would be unnecessary.

Despite the TSA's reasons, its decision angered many pilots. These pilots are trying to get the decision changed by the U.S. Congress. The pilots may get their wish. As of July 2002, the House of Representatives passed a bill allowing pilots to carry guns.

Airlines are also working to get permission for pilots to use stun guns. Stun guns are not lethal and pose no threat to the safety of the passengers.

CLASSIFIED INFORMATION

Even minutes before take-off, the Federal Aviation Administration (FAA) may assign sky marshals to a flight that it thinks is at high risk of being hijacked. The airline must allow the sky marshals on the plane. Sometimes, this last minute decision angers an airline. The airline feels it may lose customers when someone in first class is made to give up his or her seat.

They deliver an electric shock to an attacker that can immobilize him or her. However, if two or more hijackers with weapons are on a plane, a stun gun may not save anyone. This is because it takes time for a stun gun to be reloaded. Reloading takes long enough for a second hijacker to be able to attack the pilot. Stun guns can also run out of power, making them harmless.

Taking Action

For now, the TSA and the U.S. government are relying on ground security and sky marshals to protect pilots and passengers from onboard hijackers. A few times since September 11, sky marshals have had to take action. Luckily, each situation has been a false alarm and was usually just a case of an unruly passenger.

No one knows when and where a hijacking will take place. Right now, hundreds, maybe even thousands, of highly trained sky marshals are ready and waiting.

When used correctly, stun guns can be quite shocking.

New Words

applicant someone who has written formally asking for something, such as a job

background check a survey that the government or some other agency conducts to find information about a person's personal history

flight crew the people in charge of flying a plane

hijack to take illegal control of a vehicle and force its pilot or driver to go somewhere

immobilize to prevent someone from moving

international involving different countries

negotiation the process of bargaining or discussing something so that you can come to an agreement

protest to object to something strongly and publicly

ransom money that is demanded before someone who is being held captive can be set free

New Words

recruits people who have recently joined a group or an organization

requirements things that you need to do or have

scenario an outline of a series of events that might happen in a particular situation

simulate to copy or imitate

sky marshal an armed security agent who works undercover on planes

top-secret security clearance authorization to know confidential government information

undercover working as a spy without the knowledge of those under investigation; a secret investigation

Bernardo, John. *What You Can Do for Your Own Flying Safety and Security.* Bloomington, IN: 1stBooks Library, 2001.

Fridell, Ron. *Terrorism: Political Violence at Home and Abroad.* Berkeley Heights, NJ: Enslow Publishers, 2001.

Lalley, Patrick. *9.11.01: Terrorists Attack the U.S.* Chatham, NJ: Raintree Steck-Vaughn Publishers, 2002.

Meltzer, Milton. *The Day the Sky Fell: A History of Terrorism.* New York, NY: Random House Publishers, Inc., 2002.

Parker, Steve. *Airplanes.* Brookfield, CT: Millbrook Press, 1995.

Resources

Organizations

Federal Aviation Administration (FAA)
800 Independence Avenue, S.W., Room 810
Washington, D.C. 20591
www.faa.gov

Flight Safety Foundation
601 Madison Street, Suite 300
Alexandria, Virginia 22314-1756
(703) 739-6700
fax: (703) 739-6708
www.flightsafety.org/home.html

Web Sites

Aviation Safety Network
http://aviation-safety.net/database/hijackings/index.html
This site lists all hijackings attempted since 1948.
You can learn which airline was targeted, when the
hijacking took place (or was attempted), and how the
incident ended.

The National Transportation Safety Board (NTSB)
www.ntsb.gov/
This official U.S. government site has information
about airline safety and crash investigations. You can
learn how to prepare yourself for safety when flying.

Transportation Security Administration
www.tsa.gov
Learn about the TSA on its official Web site.

Index

A
applicant, 18

B
background check, 18

C
combat skills, 27
criminal investigation, 23
Cuba, 10–11, 13

F
Federal Air Marshal (FAM),
    13, 17, 20, 23, 30
Federal Aviation Authority,
    17

H
hijack, 5, 9–11, 14

N
negotiation, 23
Nixon, Richard, 11

P
Pentagon, 14
Peru, 9
pilot, 38–40

R
recruits, 23
Reagan, Ronald, 12
requirements, 18–19

S
scenario, 5, 31
shoot-house, 25
simulation training, 29
stun gun, 39–40

Index

T

terrorists, 11, 18, 35
top-secret security clearance, 18
trainee, 23, 25, 27–32

W

World Trade Center, 14

X

X-ray scanners, 35

About the Author

Mark Beyer has flown more than a quarter-million miles as an airline passenger. He has often wondered who might be a sky marshal during his flights. Mark is a writer and editor living outside New York City.